HAL•LEONARD

 JAZZ PLAY ALONG®

Book and CD for B♭, E♭, C and Bass Clef Instruments

volume 68

Produced by
Sue Mingus

CHARLES MINGUS

10 JAZZ CLASSICS

BOOK

CD

Cover photo by Bob Parent

ISBN: 978-1-4234-1703-3

HAL•LEONARD®
CORPORATION
7777 W. BLUEMOUND RD. P.O. BOX 13819 MILWAUKEE, WI 53213

Visit Hal Leonard Online at
www.halleonard.com

Charles Mingus

HAL•LEONARD

JAZZ PLAY ALONG

Volume 68

Produced by Sue Mingus

Featured Players:

Seamus Blake–Tenor Saxophone
John Hicks–Piano
Boris Kozlov–Bass
Tommy Campbell–Drums

HOW TO USE THE CD:

Each song has two tracks:

1) Melody Track

Woodwind, Brass, Keyboard, and **Mallet Players** can use
this track as a learning tool for melody style and inflection. In this
special edition of the **Hal Leonard Jazz Play Along** series, solos
are also included on this track.

2) Split Track/Accompaniment

Soloists or **Groups** can learn and perform with this
accompaniment track with the RHYTHM SECTION only.

Bass Players can learn and perform with this track –
remove the recorded bass track by turning down the
volume on the RIGHT channel.

Keyboard and **Guitar Players** can learn and perform with
this track – remove the recorded piano part by turning
down the volume on the LEFT channel.

CD

① : MELODY TRACK

② : SPLIT TRACK/ACCOMPANIMENT

BETTER GET HIT IN YOUR SOUL

BY CHARLES MINGUS

C VERSION

CD

◆3 : MELODY TRACK

◆4 : SPLIT TRACK/ACCOMPANIMENT

C VERSION

BOOGIE STOP SHUFFLE

BY CHARLES MINGUS

UPTEMPO SHUFFLE

SOLOS (9 CHORUSES)

GOODBYE PORK PIE HAT

BY CHARLES MINGUS

CD
7: MELODY TRACK
8: SPLIT TRACK/ACCOMPANIMENT

GUNSLINGING BIRD

BY CHARLES MINGUS

C VERSION

JELLY ROLL

BY CHARLES MINGUS

CD
- ◆ **9**: MELODY TRACK
- ◆ **10**: SPLIT TRACK/ACCOMPANIMENT

C VERSION

11

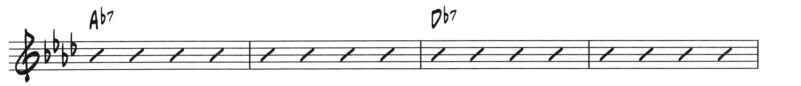

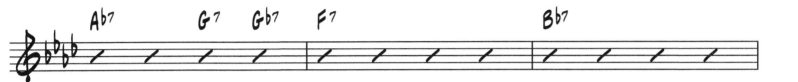

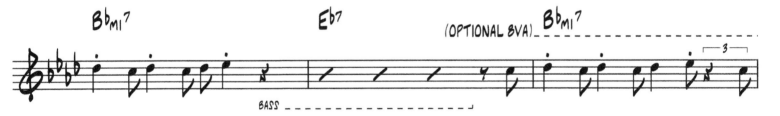

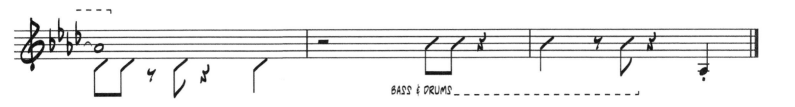

CD

NOSTALGIA IN TIMES SQUARE

BY CHARLES MINGUS

C VERSION

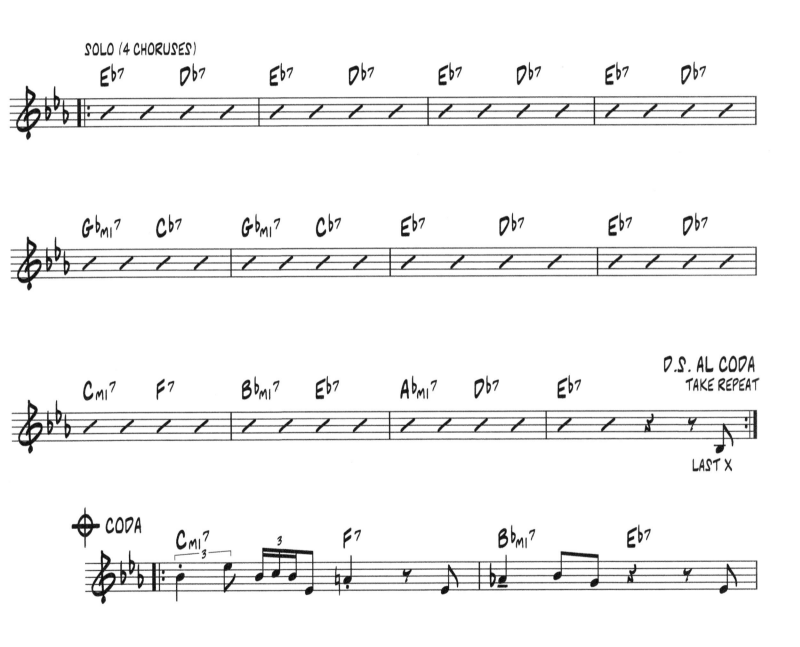

PEGGY'S BLUE SKYLIGHT

BY CHARLES MINGUS

C VERSION

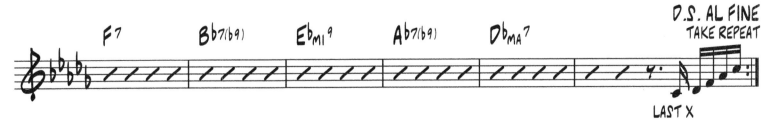

CD

15 : MELODY TRACK

16 : SPLIT TRACK/ACCOMPANIMENT

PITHECANTHROPUS ERECTUS

BY CHARLES MINGUS

C VERSION

MEDIUM SWING

TO CODA

SOLO BREAK

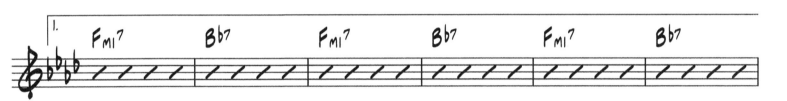

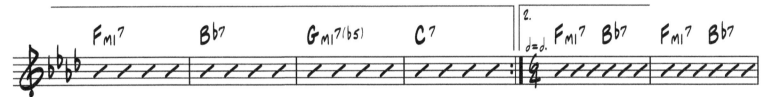

CD

PORTRAIT

C VERSION

WORDS AND MUSIC BY
CHARLES MINGUS

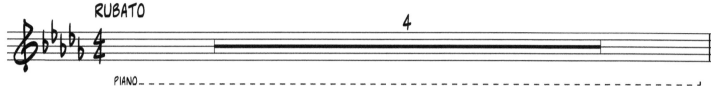

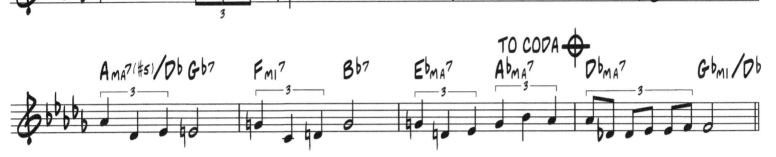

SLIPPERS

BY CHARLES MINGUS

C VERSION

SOLOS (5 CHORUSES)

Bb MA7   Ab7   Db MA7

21

C MI7   F7   Bb MA7   Db7   C MI7   F7

Bb MA7   Ab7   Db MA7

C MI7   F7   Bb MA7   Bb7

Eb MI7   Ab7   Db MA7

Eb MI7   Ab7   Db MA7   F7

Bb MA7   Ab7   Db MA7

D.S. AL CODA
TAKE REPEAT

C MI7   F7   Bb MA7   Db7   C MI7   F7

PLAY 14 X'S AD LIB.

CODA   Bb MA7   B MA7   Bb MA7

CD
❶: MELODY TRACK
❷: SPLIT TRACK/ACCOMPANIMENT

BETTER GET HIT IN YOUR SOUL

BY CHARLES MINGUS

B♭ VERSION

CD

◆ 3 : MELODY TRACK
◆ 4 : SPLIT TRACK/ACCOMPANIMENT

BOOGIE STOP SHUFFLE

BY CHARLES MINGUS

B♭ VERSION

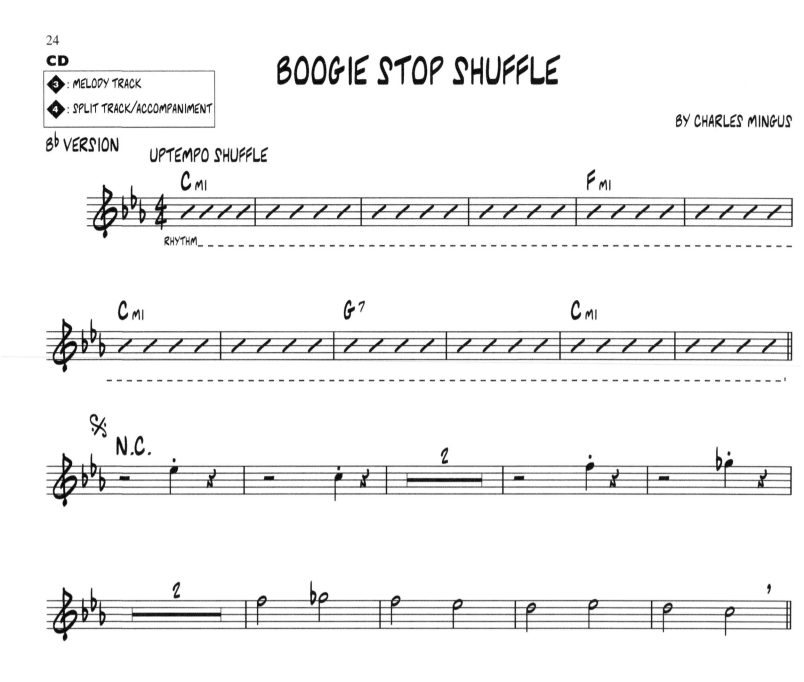

CD

◆ 5 : MELODY TRACK
◆ 6 : SPLIT TRACK/ACCOMPANIMENT

GOODBYE PORK PIE HAT

BY CHARLES MINGUS

Bb VERSION   BALLAD

GUNSLINGING BIRD

BY CHARLES MINGUS

CD

7 : MELODY TRACK

8 : SPLIT TRACK/ACCOMPANIMENT

Bb VERSION

CD
◆ **9** : MELODY TRACK
◆ **10** : SPLIT TRACK/ACCOMPANIMENT

JELLY ROLL

BY CHARLES MINGUS

B♭ VERSION   MEDIUM SWING

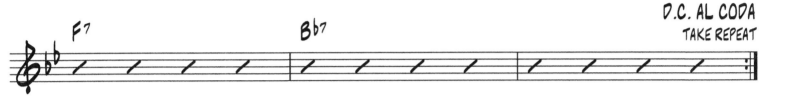

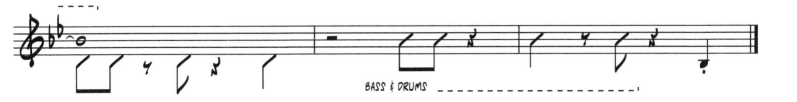

NOSTALGIA IN TIMES SQUARE

BY CHARLES MINGUS

Bb VERSION

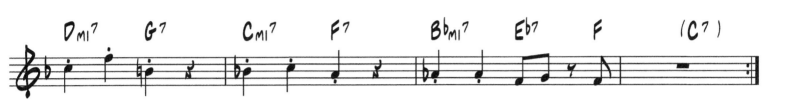

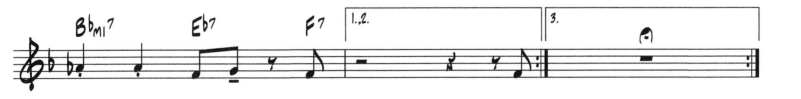

PEGGY'S BLUE SKYLIGHT

CD
- 13 : MELODY TRACK
- 14 : SPLIT TRACK/ACCOMPANIMENT

BY CHARLES MINGUS

Bb Version

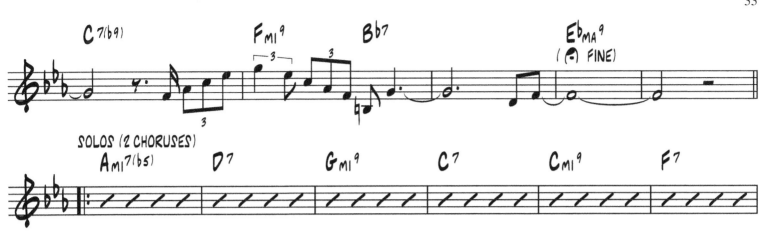

CD

15 : MELODY TRACK
16 : SPLIT TRACK/ACCOMPANIMENT

PITHECANTHROPUS ERECTUS

BY CHARLES MINGUS

Bb VERSION

MEDIUM SWING

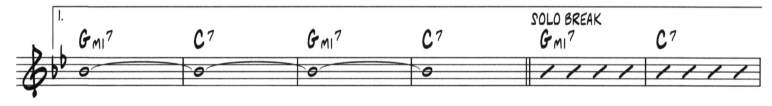

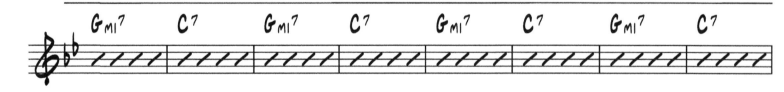

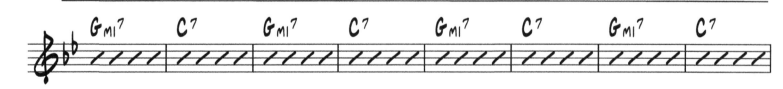

35

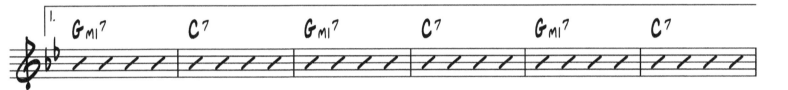

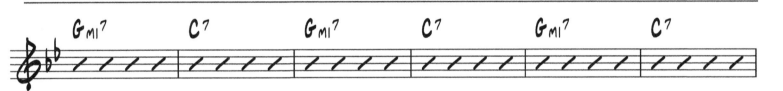

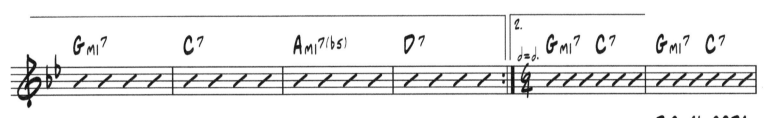

CD

PORTRAIT

WORDS AND MUSIC BY
CHARLES MINGUS

B♭ VERSION

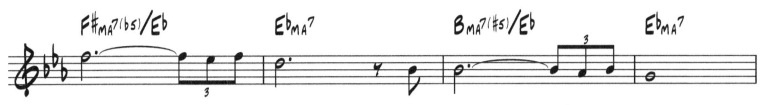

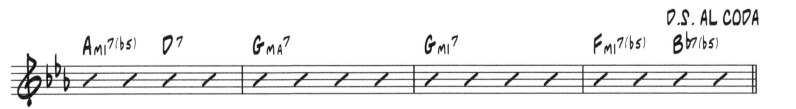

SLIPPERS

BY CHARLES MINGUS

Bb VERSION

SOLOS (5 CHORUSES)

D.S. AL CODA
TAKE REPEAT

CODA
PLAY 14 X'S AD LIB.

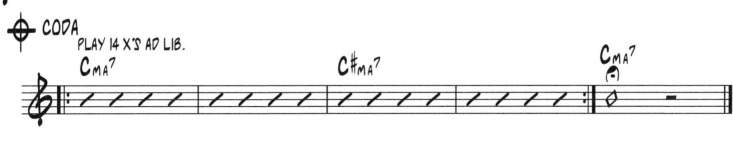

CD
◆1: MELODY TRACK
◆2: SPLIT TRACK/ACCOMPANIMENT

BETTER GET HIT IN YOUR SOUL

BY CHARLES MINGUS

E♭ VERSION

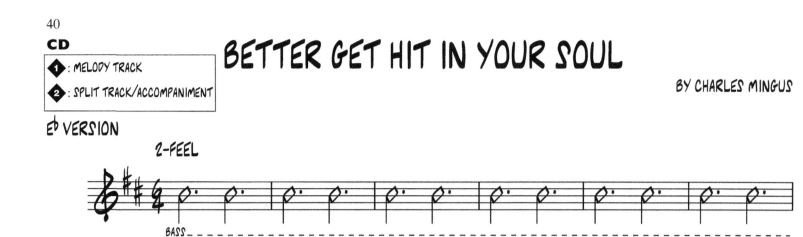

CD
- ❸: MELODY TRACK
- ❹: SPLIT TRACK/ACCOMPANIMENT

BOOGIE STOP SHUFFLE

BY CHARLES MINGUS

E♭ VERSION

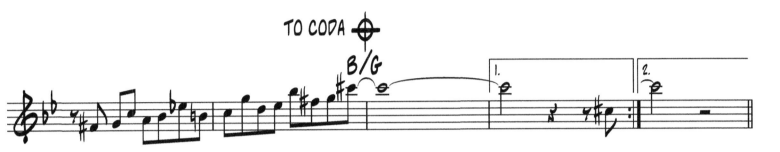

GOODBYE PORK PIE HAT

BY CHARLES MINGUS

E♭ VERSION

(PLAY C♯ ON D.S.)

TO CODA ⊕

SOLOS (PLAY 2 X'S)

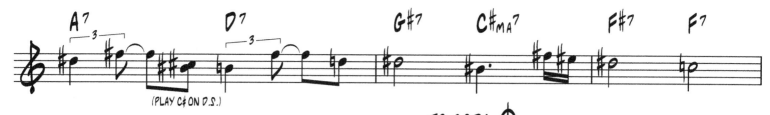

D.S. AL CODA

LAST XO

⊕ CODA

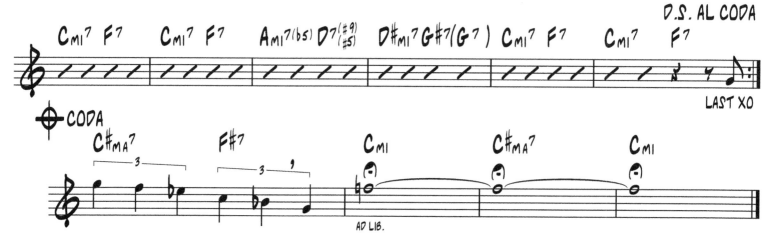

AD LIB.

GUNSLINGING BIRD

BY CHARLES MINGUS

CD
◆ 9 : MELODY TRACK
◆ 10 : SPLIT TRACK/ACCOMPANIMENT

JELLY ROLL

BY CHARLES MINGUS

E♭ VERSION

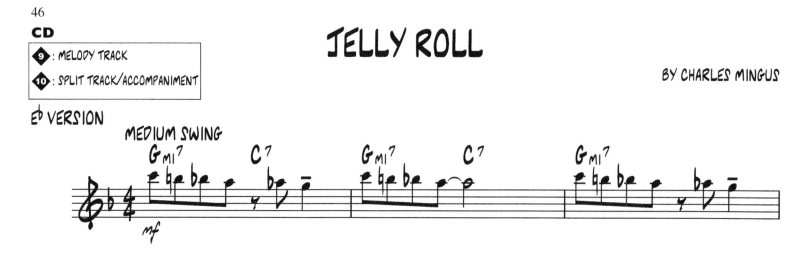

F7　　　　　　　　　　Bb7

F7　E7　Eb7　D7　　　G7

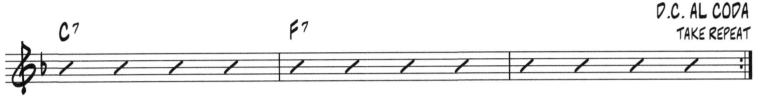

C7　　　F7　　　D.C. AL CODA / TAKE REPEAT

CODA C7(#9)(#5)　F　C7(#9)(#5)　F

DRUMS _ _ _ _ _ _

Gmi7　　　C7

BASS _ _ _ _ _ _

Gmi7　　C7　　Gmi7

BASS _ _ _ _ _ _

C7　　　　　F7

BASS & DRUMS _ _ _ _ _ _

CD
- 11 : MELODY TRACK
- 12 : SPLIT TRACK/ACCOMPANIMENT

NOSTALGIA IN TIMES SQUARE

BY CHARLES MINGUS

E♭ VERSION

49

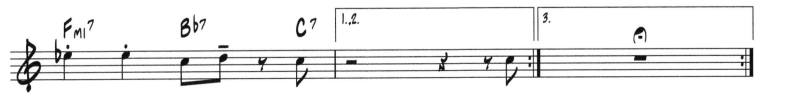

CD

◆13: MELODY TRACK

◆14: SPLIT TRACK/ACCOMPANIMENT

PEGGY'S BLUE SKYLIGHT

BY CHARLES MINGUS

E♭ VERSION

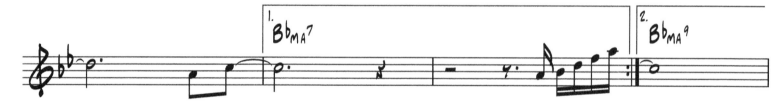

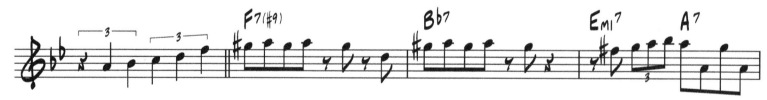

G7(b9)　　　　　Cmi9　　　　F7　　　　　　Bbma9
(⌒ FINE)

SOLOS (2 CHORUSES)

Emi7(b5)　A7　　Dmi9　　G7　　Gmi9　　C7

Fma9　　B7　　Bb7sus　　A7　　D7　　G7(b9)

Cmi9　　F7(b9)　　Bbma7　　　　Emi7(b5)　A7

Dmi9　　G7　　Gmi9　　C7　　Fma9　　B7

Bb7sus　A7　　D7　　G7(b9)　　Cmi9　　F7(b5)

Bbma7　　　　F7　　Bb7　　Emi7　A7　　Dma7

Dmi7(b5)　G7(b9)　Cma7　　Fma7 B7　Bb7sus　A7

D7　　G7(b9)　Cmi9　　F7(b9)　　Bbma7

D.S. AL FINE
TAKE REPEAT

LAST X

CD

15 : MELODY TRACK
16 : SPLIT TRACK/ACCOMPANIMENT

PITHECANTHROPUS ERECTUS

BY CHARLES MINGUS

E♭ VERSION

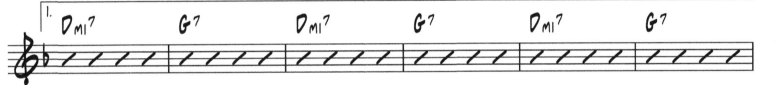

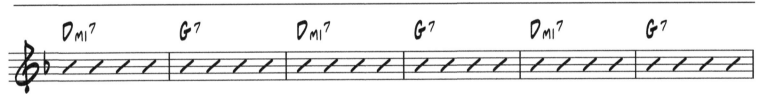

CD

17 : MELODY TRACK

18 : SPLIT TRACK/ACCOMPANIMENT

PORTRAIT

WORDS AND MUSIC BY
CHARLES MINGUS

E♭ VERSION

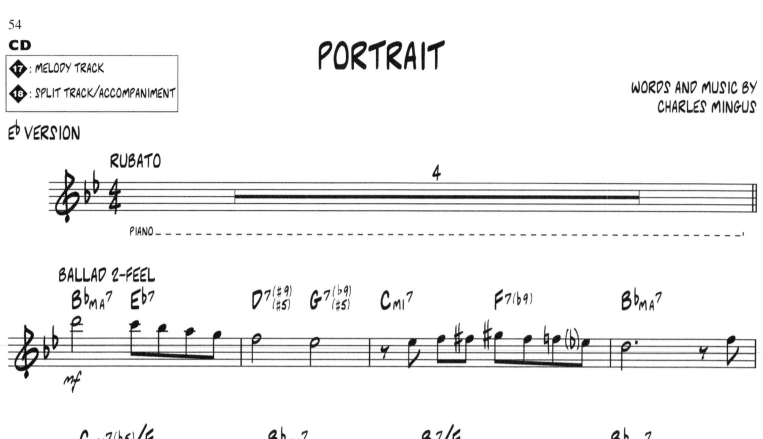

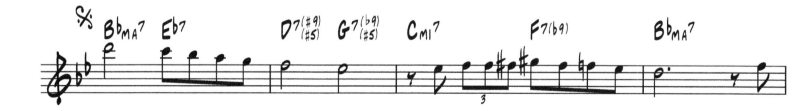

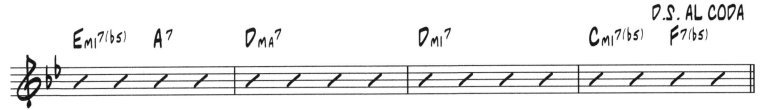

SLIPPERS

BY CHARLES MINGUS

CD
- **19**: MELODY TRACK
- **20**: SPLIT TRACK/ACCOMPANIMENT

Eb VERSION

UPTEMPO SWING

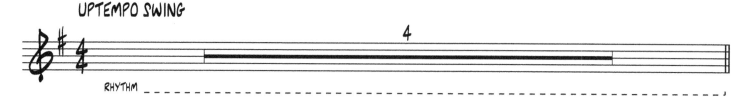

RHYTHM

TO CODA ⊕

57

SOLOS (5 CHORUSES)

Gma7 | F7 | Bbma7 | |

Ami7 | D7 | Gma7 Bb7 | Ami7 D7 |

Gma7 | F7 | Bbma7 | |

Ami7 | D7 | Gma7 | G7 |

Cmi7 | F7 | Bbma7 | |

Cmi7 | F7 | Bbma7 | D7 |

Gma7 | F7 | Bbma7 | |

D.S. AL CODA
TAKE REPEAT

Ami7 | D7 | Gma7 Bb7 | Ami7 D7 |

CODA PLAY 14 X'S AD LIB.

Gma7 | | G#ma7 | | Gma7

CD

① : MELODY TRACK
② : SPLIT TRACK/ACCOMPANIMENT

BETTER GET HIT IN YOUR SOUL

BY CHARLES MINGUS

𝄢: C VERSION

2-FEEL

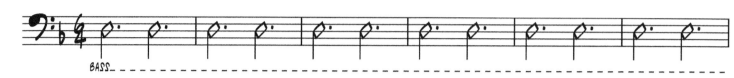

59

BOOGIE STOP SHUFFLE

CD
- ❸ : MELODY TRACK
- ❹ : SPLIT TRACK/ACCOMPANIMENT

BY CHARLES MINGUS

𝄢 C VERSION

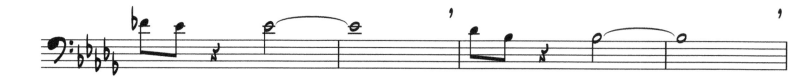

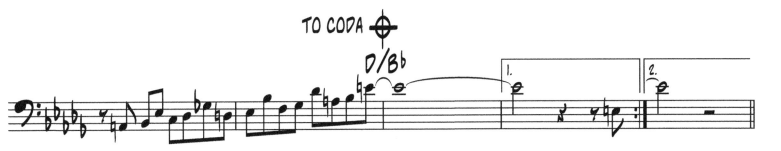

SOLOS (9 CHORUSES)

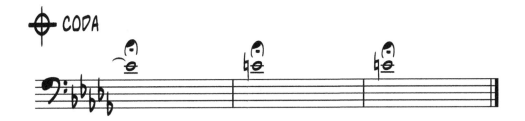

CD
◆5: MELODY TRACK
◆6: SPLIT TRACK/ACCOMPANIMENT

GOODBYE PORK PIE HAT

BY CHARLES MINGUS

𝄢: C VERSION

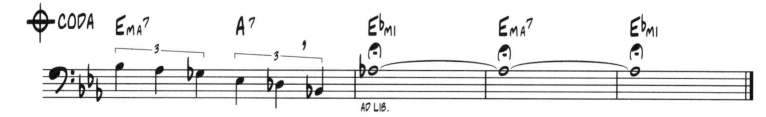

GUNSLINGING BIRD

BY CHARLES MINGUS

CD

◆9: MELODY TRACK
◆10: SPLIT TRACK/ACCOMPANIMENT

JELLY ROLL

BY CHARLES MINGUS

𝄢: C VERSION

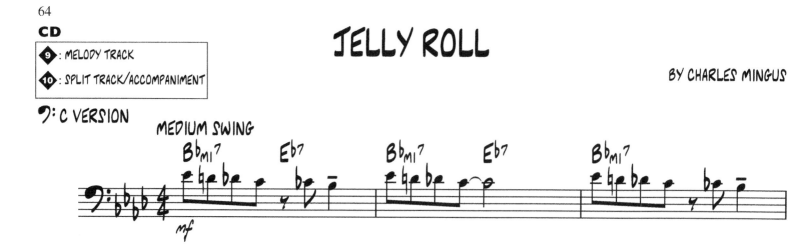

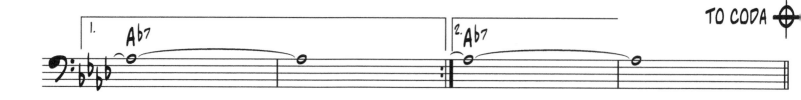

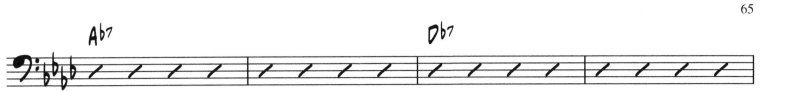

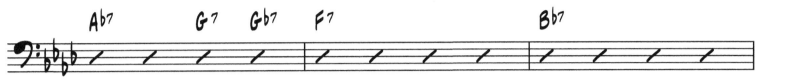

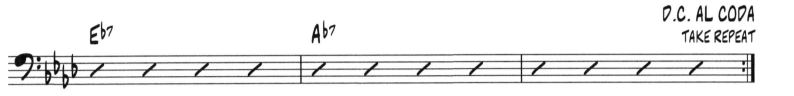

NOSTALGIA IN TIMES SQUARE

CD
🎵 11 : MELODY TRACK
🎵 12 : SPLIT TRACK/ACCOMPANIMENT

𝄢 : C VERSION

BY CHARLES MINGUS

MEDIUM SWING

OPTIONAL SOLO BREAK NEXT 12 BARS

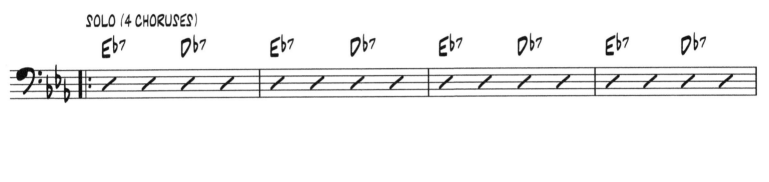

SOLO (4 CHORUSES)

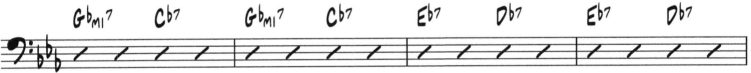

D.S. AL CODA
TAKE REPEAT

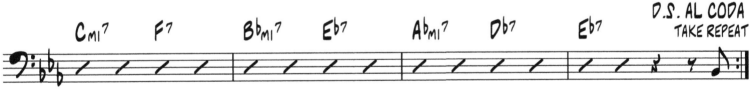

LAST X

PEGGY'S BLUE SKYLIGHT

BY CHARLES MINGUS

Bb7(b9)   Ebmi9   Ab7   Dbma9
(⌢ FINE)

SOLOS (2 CHORUSES)
Gmi7(b5)   C7   Fmi9   Bb7   Bbmi9   Eb7

Abma9   D7   Db7sus   C7   F7   Bb7(b9)

Ebmi9   Ab7(b9)   Dbma7   Gmi7(b5)   C7

Fmi9   Bb7   Bbmi9   Eb7   Abma9   D7

Db7sus   C7   F7   Bb7(b9)   Ebmi9   Ab7(b5)

Dbma7   Ab7   Db7   Gmi7 C7   Fma7

Fmi7(b5)   Bb7(b9)   Ebma7   Abma7 D7   Db7sus   C7

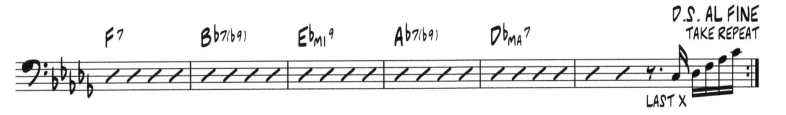

D.S. AL FINE
TAKE REPEAT
F7   Bb7(b9)   Ebmi9   Ab7(b9)   Dbma7
LAST X

CD

◆15◆ : MELODY TRACK

◆16◆ : SPLIT TRACK/ACCOMPANIMENT

PITHECANTHROPUS ERECTUS

BY CHARLES MINGUS

𝄢 : C VERSION

71

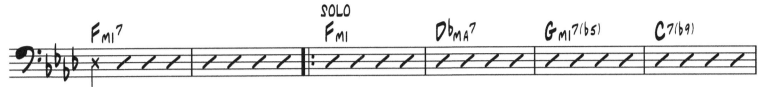

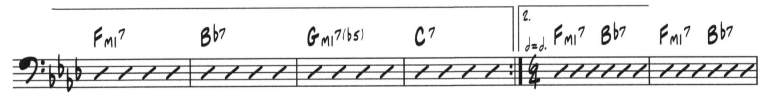

CD

17 : MELODY TRACK
18 : SPLIT TRACK/ACCOMPANIMENT

𝄢 C VERSION

PORTRAIT

WORDS AND MUSIC BY
CHARLES MINGUS

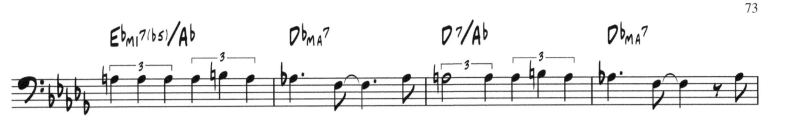

CD

19 : MELODY TRACK

20 : SPLIT TRACK/ACCOMPANIMENT

SLIPPERS

BY CHARLES MINGUS

𝄢: C VERSION

SOLOS (5 CHORUSES)

Bb MA7   Ab7   Db MA7

Cmi7   F7   Bb MA7   Db7   Cmi7   F7

Bb MA7   Ab7   Db MA7

Cmi7   F7   Bb MA7   Bb7

Eb mi7   Ab7   Db MA7

Eb mi7   Ab7   Db MA7   F7

Bb MA7   Ab7   Db MA7

D.S. AL CODA
TAKE REPEAT

Cmi7   F7   Bb MA7   Db7   Cmi7   F7

⊕ CODA   PLAY 14 X'S AD LIB.

Bb MA7   B MA7   Bb MA7
                                                   (–)

Presenting the Hal Leonard JAZZ PLAY-ALONG SERIES

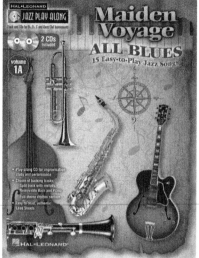

For use with all B-flat, E-flat, Bass Clef and C instruments, the Jazz Play-Along® Series is the ultimate learning tool for all jazz musicians. With musician-friendly lead sheets, melody cues, and other split-track audio choices included, these first-of-a-kind packages help you master improvisation while playing some of the greatest tunes of all time. FOR STUDY, each tune includes a split track with: melody cue with proper style and inflection • professional rhythm tracks • choruses for soloing • removable bass part • removable piano part. FOR PERFORMANCE, each tune also has: an additional full stereo accompaniment track (no melody) • additional choruses for soloing.

1A. MAIDEN VOYAGE/ALL BLUES
00843158 .... $22.99

1. DUKE ELLINGTON
00841644 .... $16.99

2. MILES DAVIS
00841645 .... $17.99

3. THE BLUES
00841646 .... $19.99

4. JAZZ BALLADS
00841691 .... $17.99

5. BEST OF BEBOP
00841689 .... $17.99

6. JAZZ CLASSICS WITH EASY CHANGES
00841690 .... $16.99

7. ESSENTIAL JAZZ STANDARDS
00843000 .... $17.99

8. ANTONIO CARLOS JOBIM AND THE ART OF THE BOSSA NOVA
00843001 .... $16.99

9. DIZZY GILLESPIE
00843002 .... $19.99

10. DISNEY CLASSICS
00843003 .... $16.99

12. ESSENTIAL JAZZ CLASSICS
00843005 .... $16.99

13. JOHN COLTRANE
00843006 .... $17.99

14. IRVING BERLIN
00843007 .... $16.99

15. RODGERS & HAMMERSTEIN
00843008 .... $16.99

16. COLE PORTER
00843009 .... $17.99

17. COUNT BASIE
00843010 .... $17.99

18. HAROLD ARLEN
00843011 .... $17.99

20. CHRISTMAS CAROLS
00843080 .... $16.99

21. RODGERS AND HART CLASSICS
00843014 .... $16.99

22. WAYNE SHORTER
00843015 .... $17.99

23. LATIN JAZZ
00843016 .... $19.99

24. EARLY JAZZ STANDARDS
00843017 .... $16.99

25. CHRISTMAS JAZZ
00843018 .... $17.99

26. CHARLIE PARKER
00843019 .... $16.99

27. GREAT JAZZ STANDARDS
00843020 .... $17.99

28. BIG BAND ERA
00843021 .... $17.99

29. LENNON AND MCCARTNEY
00843022 .... $24.99

30. BLUES' BEST
00843023 .... $16.99

31. JAZZ IN THREE
00843024 .... $16.99

32. BEST OF SWING
00843025 .... $17.99

33. SONNY ROLLINS
00843029 .... $16.99

34. ALL TIME STANDARDS
00843030 .... $17.99

35. BLUESY JAZZ
00843031 .... $17.99

36. HORACE SILVER
00843032 .... $19.99

37. BILL EVANS
00843033 .... $16.99

38. YULETIDE JAZZ
00843034 .... $16.99

39. "ALL THE THINGS YOU ARE" & MORE JEROME KERN SONGS
00843035 .... $19.99

40. BOSSA NOVA
00843036 .... $19.99

41. CLASSIC DUKE ELLINGTON
00843037 .... $16.99

42. GERRY MULLIGAN FAVORITES
00843038 .... $16.99

43. GERRY MULLIGAN CLASSICS
00843039 .... $19.99

45. GEORGE GERSHWIN
00103643 .... $24.99

47. CLASSIC JAZZ BALLADS
00843043 .... $17.99

48. BEBOP CLASSICS
00843044 .... $16.99

49. MILES DAVIS STANDARDS
00843045 .... $19.99

52. STEVIE WONDER
00843048 .... $17.99

53. RHYTHM CHANGES
00843049 .... $16.99

55. BENNY GOLSON
00843052 .... $19.99

56. "GEORGIA ON MY MIND" & OTHER SONGS BY HOAGY CARMICHAEL
00843056 .... $17.99

57. VINCE GUARALDI
00843057 .... $16.99

58. MORE LENNON AND MCCARTNEY
00843059 .... $17.99

59. SOUL JAZZ
00843060 .... $17.99

60. DEXTER GORDON
00843061 .... $16.99

61. MONGO SANTAMARIA
00843062 .... $16.99

62. JAZZ-ROCK FUSION
00843063 .... $19.99

63. CLASSICAL JAZZ
00843064 .... $16.99

64. TV TUNES
00843065 .... $16.99

65. SMOOTH JAZZ
00843066 .... $19.99

66. A CHARLIE BROWN CHRISTMAS
00843067 .... $16.99

67. CHICK COREA
00843068 .... $22.99

68. CHARLES MINGUS
00843069 .... $19.99

71. COLE PORTER CLASSICS
00843073 .... $16.99

72. CLASSIC JAZZ BALLADS
00843074 .... $16.99

73. JAZZ/BLUES
00843075 .... $16.99

74. BEST JAZZ CLASSICS
00843076 .... $16.99

75. PAUL DESMOND
00843077 .... $17.99

78. STEELY DAN
00843070 .... $19.99

79. MILES DAVIS CLASSICS
00843081 .... $16.99

80. JIMI HENDRIX
00843083 .... $17.99

83. ANDREW LLOYD WEBBER
00843104 .... $16.99

84. BOSSA NOVA CLASSICS
00843105 .... $17.99

85. MOTOWN HITS
00843109 .... $17.99

86. BENNY GOODMAN
00843110 .... $17.99

87. DIXIELAND
00843111 .... $16.99

90. **THELONIOUS MONK CLASSICS**
   00841262 ....$16.99

91. **THELONIOUS MONK FAVORITES**
   00841263 ....$17.99

92. **LEONARD BERNSTEIN**
   00450134 ....$16.99

93. **DISNEY FAVORITES**
   00843142 ....$16.99

94. **RAY**
   00843143 ....$19.99

95. **JAZZ AT THE LOUNGE**
   00843144 ....$17.99

96. **LATIN JAZZ STANDARDS**
   00843145 ....$16.99

97. **MAYBE I'M AMAZED***
   00843148 ....$16.99

98. **DAVE FRISHBERG**
   00843149 ....$16.99

99. **SWINGING STANDARDS**
   00843150 ....$16.99

100. **LOUIS ARMSTRONG**
   00740423 ....$19.99

101. **BUD POWELL**
   00843152 ....$16.99

102. **JAZZ POP**
   00843153 ....$19.99

103. **ON GREEN DOLPHIN STREET
   & OTHER JAZZ CLASSICS**
   00843154 ....$16.99

104. **ELTON JOHN**
   00843155 ....$19.99

105. **SOULFUL JAZZ**
   00843151 ....$17.99

106. **SLO' JAZZ**
   00843117 ....$16.99

107. **MOTOWN CLASSICS**
   00843116 ....$17.99

108. **JAZZ WALTZ**
   00843159 ....$16.99

109. **OSCAR PETERSON**
   00843160 ....$16.99

110. **JUST STANDARDS**
   00843161 ....$16.99

111. **COOL CHRISTMAS**
   00843162 ....$16.99

112. **PAQUITO D'RIVERA – LATIN JAZZ***
   48020662 ....$16.99

113. **PAQUITO D'RIVERA – BRAZILIAN JAZZ***
   48020663 ....$19.99

114. **MODERN JAZZ QUARTET FAVORITES**
   00843163 ....$16.99

115. **THE SOUND OF MUSIC**
   00843164 ....$16.99

116. **JACO PASTORIUS**
   00843165 ....$17.99

117. **ANTONIO CARLOS JOBIM – MORE HITS**
   00843166 ....$17.99

118. **BIG JAZZ STANDARDS COLLECTION**
   00843167 ....$27.50

119. **JELLY ROLL MORTON**
   00843168 ....$16.99

120. **J.S. BACH**
   00843169 ....$17.99

121. **DJANGO REINHARDT**
   00843170 ....$16.99

122. **PAUL SIMON**
   00843182 ....$16.99

123. **BACHARACH & DAVID**
   00843185 ....$16.99

124. **JAZZ-ROCK HORN HITS**
   00843186 ....$16.99

125. **SAMMY NESTICO**
   00843187 ....$16.99

126. **COUNT BASIE CLASSICS**
   00843157 ....$16.99

127. **CHUCK MANGIONE**
   00843188 ....$19.99

128. **VOCAL STANDARDS (LOW VOICE)**
   00843189 ....$16.99

129. **VOCAL STANDARDS (HIGH VOICE)**
   00843190 ....$16.99

130. **VOCAL JAZZ (LOW VOICE)**
   00843191 ....$16.99

131. **VOCAL JAZZ (HIGH VOICE)**
   00843192 ....$16.99

132. **STAN GETZ ESSENTIALS**
   00843193 ....$17.99

133. **STAN GETZ FAVORITES**
   00843194 ....$16.99

134. **NURSERY RHYMES***
   00843196 ....$17.99

135. **JEFF BECK**
   00843197 ....$16.99

136. **NAT ADDERLEY**
   00843198 ....$16.99

137. **WES MONTGOMERY**
   00843199 ....$16.99

138. **FREDDIE HUBBARD**
   00843200 ....$16.99

139. **JULIAN "CANNONBALL" ADDERLEY**
   00843201 ....$16.99

140. **JOE ZAWINUL**
   00843202 ....$16.99

141. **BILL EVANS STANDARDS**
   00843156 ....$16.99

142. **CHARLIE PARKER GEMS**
   00843222 ....$16.99

143. **JUST THE BLUES**
   00843223 ....$16.99

144. **LEE MORGAN**
   00843229 ....$16.99

145. **COUNTRY STANDARDS**
   00843230 ....$16.99

146. **RAMSEY LEWIS**
   00843231 ....$16.99

147. **SAMBA**
   00843232 ....$16.99

148. **JOHN COLTRANE FAVORITES**
   00843233 ....$16.99

149. **JOHN COLTRANE – GIANT STEPS**
   00843234 ....$16.99

150. **JAZZ IMPROV BASICS**
   00843195 ....$19.99

151. **MODERN JAZZ QUARTET CLASSICS**
   00843209 ....$16.99

152. **J.J. JOHNSON**
   00843210 ....$16.99

153. **KENNY GARRETT**
   00843212 ....$16.99

154. **HENRY MANCINI**
   00843213 ....$17.99

155. **SMOOTH JAZZ CLASSICS**
   00843215 ....$17.99

156. **THELONIOUS MONK – EARLY GEMS**
   00843216 ....$16.99

157. **HYMNS**
   00843217 ....$16.99

158. **JAZZ COVERS ROCK**
   00843219 ....$16.99

159. **MOZART**
   00843220 ....$16.99

160. **GEORGE SHEARING**
   14041531 ....$16.99

161. **DAVE BRUBECK**
   14041556 ....$16.99

162. **BIG CHRISTMAS COLLECTION**
   00843221 ....$24.99

163. **JOHN COLTRANE STANDARDS**
   00843235 ....$16.99

164. **HERB ALPERT**
   14041775 ....$19.99

165. **GEORGE BENSON**
   00843240 ....$17.99

166. **ORNETTE COLEMAN**
   00843241 ....$16.99

167. **JOHNNY MANDEL**
   00103642 ....$16.99

168. **TADD DAMERON**
   00103663 ....$16.99

169. **BEST JAZZ STANDARDS**
   00109249 ....$24.99

170. **ULTIMATE JAZZ STANDARDS**
   00109250 ....$24.99

171. **RADIOHEAD**
   00109305 ....$16.99

172. **POP STANDARDS**
   00111669 ....$16.99

174. **TIN PAN ALLEY**
   00119125 ....$16.99

175. **TANGO**
   00119836 ....$16.99

176. **JOHNNY MERCER**
   00119838 ....$16.99

177. **THE II-V-I PROGRESSION**
   00843239 ....$24.99

178. **JAZZ/FUNK**
   00121902 ....$17.99

179. **MODAL JAZZ**
   00122273 ....$16.99

180. **MICHAEL JACKSON**
   00122327 ....$17.99

181. **BILLY JOEL**
   00122329 ....$19.99

182. **"RHAPSODY IN BLUE" & 7 OTHER
   CLASSICAL-BASED JAZZ PIECES**
   00116847 ....$16.99

183. **SONDHEIM**
   00126253 ....$16.99

184. **JIMMY SMITH**
   00126943 ....$17.99

185. **JAZZ FUSION**
   00127558 ....$17.99

186. **JOE PASS**
   00128391 ....$16.99

187. **CHRISTMAS FAVORITES**
   00128393 ....$16.99

188. **PIAZZOLLA – 10 FAVORITE TUNES**
   48023253 ....$16.99

189. **JOHN LENNON**
   00138678 ....$16.99

*These do not include split tracks.

ARTIST TRANSCRIPTIONS

Artist Transcriptions are authentic, note-for-note transcriptions of today's hottest artists in jazz, pop and rock. These outstanding, accurate arrangements are in an easy-to-read format which includes all essential lines. **Artist Transcriptions** can be used to perform, sequence or for reference.

FLUTE

00672379	Eric Dolphy Collection	$19.95
00672582	The Very Best of James Galway	$19.99
00672372	James Moody Collection – Sax and Flute	$19.95

GUITAR & BASS

00660113	Guitar Style of George Benson	$19.99
00672573	Ray Brown – Legendary Jazz Bassist	$22.99
00672331	Ron Carter Collection	$24.99
00660115	Al Di Meola – Friday Night in San Francisco	$24.99
00125617	Best of Herb Ellis	$19.99
00699306	Jim Hall – Exploring Jazz Guitar	$19.99
00672353	The Joe Pass Collection	$22.99
00673216	John Patitucci	$22.99
00672374	Johnny Smith – Guitar Solos	$24.99

PIANO & KEYBOARD

00672487	Monty Alexander Plays Standards	$19.95
00672520	Count Basie Collection	$19.95
00192307	Bebop Piano Legends	$19.99
00113680	Blues Piano Legends	$22.99
00672526	The Bill Charlap Collection	$19.99
00278003	A Charlie Brown Christmas	$19.99
00672300	Chick Corea – Paint the World	$19.99
00146105	Bill Evans – Alone	$21.99
00672548	The Mastery of Bill Evans	$16.99
00672365	Bill Evans – Play Standards	$22.99
00121885	Bill Evans – Time Remembered	$22.99
00672510	Bill Evans Trio Vol. 1: 1959-1961	$29.99
00672511	Bill Evans Trio Vol. 2: 1962-1965	$27.99
00672512	Bill Evans Trio Vol. 3: 1968-1974	$29.99
00672513	Bill Evans Trio Vol. 4: 1979-1980	$24.95
00193332	Erroll Garner – Concert by the Sea	$22.99
00672486	Vince Guaraldi Collection	$19.99
00289644	The Definitive Vince Guaraldi	$39.99
00672419	Herbie Hancock Collection	$22.99
00672438	Hampton Hawes Collection	$19.95
00672322	Ahmad Jamal Collection	$27.99
00255671	Jazz Piano Masterpieces	$22.99
00124367	Jazz Piano Masters Play Rodgers & Hammerstein	$19.99
00672564	Best of Jeff Lorber	$19.99

00672476	Brad Mehldau Collection	$24.99
00672388	Best of Thelonious Monk	$22.99
00672389	Thelonious Monk Collection	$24.99
00672390	Thelonious Monk Plays Jazz Standards – Volume 1	$24.99
00672391	Thelonious Monk Plays Jazz Standards – Volume 2	$24.99
00672433	Jelly Roll Morton – The Piano Rolls	$19.99
00264094	Oscar Peterson – Night Train	$19.99
00672544	Oscar Peterson – Originals	$15.99
00672531	Oscar Peterson – Plays Duke Ellington	$27.99
00672563	Oscar Peterson – A Royal Wedding Suite	$19.99
00672569	Oscar Peterson – Tracks	$19.99
00672533	Oscar Peterson – Trios	$39.99
00672534	Very Best of Oscar Peterson	$27.99
00672371	Bud Powell Classics	$22.99
00672376	Bud Powell Collection	$24.99
00672507	Gonzalo Rubalcaba Collection	$19.95
00672303	Horace Silver Collection	$24.99
00672316	Art Tatum Collection	$27.99
00672355	Art Tatum Solo Book	$22.99
00672357	The Billy Taylor Collection	$24.95
00673215	McCoy Tyner	$22.99
00672321	Cedar Walton Collection	$19.95
00672519	Kenny Werner Collection	$19.95

SAXOPHONE

00672566	The Mindi Abair Collection	$14.99
00673244	Julian "Cannonball" Adderley Collection	$22.99
00673237	Michael Brecker	$24.99
00672429	Michael Brecker Collection	$24.99
00672529	John Coltrane – Giant Steps	$22.99
00672494	John Coltrane – A Love Supreme	$17.99
00672493	John Coltrane Plays "Coltrane Changes"	$19.95
00672453	John Coltrane Plays Standards	$24.99
00673233	John Coltrane Solos	$29.99
00672328	Paul Desmond Collection	$22.99
00672530	Kenny Garrett Collection	$24.99
00699375	Stan Getz	$19.99
00672377	Stan Getz – Bossa Novas	$24.99
00673254	Great Tenor Sax Solos	$22.99

00672523	Coleman Hawkins Collection	$24.99
00672330	Best of Joe Henderson	$24.99
00673239	Best of Kenny G	$22.99
00673229	Kenny G – Breathless	$19.99
00672462	Kenny G – Classics in the Key of G	$24.99
00672485	Kenny G – Faith: A Holiday Album	$17.99
00672373	Kenny G – The Moment	$22.99
00672498	Jackie McLean Collection	$19.95
00672372	James Moody Collection – Sax and Flute	$19.95
00672539	Gerry Mulligan Collection	$24.99
00102751	Sonny Rollins, Art Blakey & Kenny Drew with the Modern Jazz Quartet	$17.99
00675000	David Sanborn Collection	$19.99
00672491	The New Best of Wayne Shorter	$24.99
00672550	The Sonny Stitt Collection	$19.95
00672524	Lester Young Collection	$22.99

TROMBONE

00672332	J.J. Johnson Collection	$24.99
00672489	Steve Turré Collection	$19.99

TRUMPET

00672557	Herb Alpert Collection	$19.99
00672480	Louis Armstrong Collection	$19.99
00672481	Louis Armstrong Plays Standards	$19.99
00672435	Chet Baker Collection	$24.99
00672556	Best of Chris Botti	$19.99
00672448	Miles Davis – Originals, Vol. 1	$19.99
00672451	Miles Davis – Originals, Vol. 2	$19.95
00672449	Miles Davis – Standards, Vol. 2	$19.95
00672479	Dizzy Gillespie Collection	$19.95
00673214	Freddie Hubbard	$19.99
00672506	Chuck Mangione Collection	$22.99
00672525	Arturo Sandoval – Trumpet Evolution	$19.99

HAL•LEONARD®

Visit our web site for songlists or to order online from your favorite music retailer at
www.halleonard.com

JAZZ INSTRUCTION & IMPROVISATION
BOOKS FOR ALL INSTRUMENTS FROM HAL LEONARD

500 JAZZ LICKS
by Brent Vaartstra
This book aims to assist you on your journey to play jazz fluently. These short phrases and ideas we call "licks" will help you understand how to navigate the common chords and chord progressions you will encounter. Adding this vocabulary to your arsenal will send you down the right path and improve your jazz playing, regardless of your instrument.
00142384 ....$16.99

1001 JAZZ LICKS
by Jack Shneidman
Cherry Lane Music
This book presents 1,001 melodic gems played over dozens of the most important chord progressions heard in jazz. This is the ideal book for beginners seeking a well-organized, easy-to-follow encyclopedia of jazz vocabulary, as well as professionals who want to take their knowledge of the jazz language to new heights.
02500133 ....$17.99

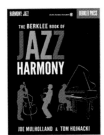

THE BERKLEE BOOK OF JAZZ HARMONY
by Joe Mulholland & Tom Hojnacki
Learn jazz harmony, as taught at Berklee College of Music. This text provides a strong foundation in harmonic principles, supporting further study in jazz composition, arranging, and improvisation. It covers basic chord types and their tensions, with practical demonstrations of how they are used in characteristic jazz contexts and an accompanying recording that lets you hear how they can be applied.
00113755 Book/Online Audio.................$34.99

BUILDING A JAZZ VOCABULARY
By Mike Steinel
A valuable resource for learning the basics of jazz from Mike Steinel of the University of North Texas. It covers: the basics of jazz • how to build effective solos • a comprehensive practice routine • and a jazz vocabulary of the masters.
00849911 ....$22.99

COMPREHENSIVE TECHNIQUE FOR JAZZ MUSICIANS
2ND EDITION
by Bert Ligon
Houston Publishing
An incredible presentation of the most practical exercises an aspiring jazz student could want. All are logically interwoven with fine "real world" examples from jazz to classical. This book is an essential anthology of technical, compositional, and theoretical exercises, with lots of musical examples.
00030455 ....$34.99

EAR TRAINING
by Keith Wyatt, Carl Schroeder and Joe Elliott
Musicians Institute Press
Covers: basic pitch matching • singing major and minor scales • identifying intervals • transcribing melodies and rhythm • identifying chords and progressions • seventh chords and the blues • modal interchange, chromaticism, modulation • and more.
00695198 Book/Online Audio.................$29.99

EXERCISES AND ETUDES FOR THE JAZZ INSTRUMENTALIST
by J.J. Johnson
Designed as study material and playable by any instrument, these pieces run the gamut of the jazz experience, featuring common and uncommon time signatures and keys, and styles from ballads to funk. They are progressively graded so that both beginners and professionals will be challenged by the demands of this wonderful music.
00842018 Bass Clef Edition $22.99
00842042 Treble Clef Edition $16.95

HOW TO PLAY FROM A REAL BOOK
by Robert Rawlins
Explore, understand, and perform the songs in real books with the techniques in this book. Learn how to analyze the form and harmonic structure, insert an introduction, interpret the melody, improvise on the chords, construct bass lines, voice the chords, add substitutions, and more. It addresses many aspects of solo and small band performance that can improve your own playing and your understanding of what others are doing around you.
00312097 ....$19.99

JAZZ DUETS
ETUDES FOR PHRASING AND ARTICULATION
by Richard Lowell
Berklee Press
With these 27 duets in jazz and jazz-influenced styles, you will learn how to improve your ear, sense of timing, phrasing, and your facility in bringing theoretical principles into musical expression. Covers: jazz staccato & legato • scales, modes & harmonies • phrasing within and between measures • swing feel • and more.
00302151 ....$14.99

JAZZ THEORY & WORKBOOK
by Lilian Dericq & Étienne Guéreau
Designed for all instrumentalists, this book teaches how jazz standards are constructed. It is also a great resource for arrangers and composers seeking new writing tools. While some of the musical examples are pianistic, this book is not exclusively for keyboard players.
00159022 ....$19.99

JAZZ THEORY RESOURCES
by Bert Ligon
Houston Publishing, Inc.
This is a jazz theory text in two volumes. **Volume 1 includes**: review of basic theory • rhythm in jazz performance • triadic generalization • diatonic harmonic progressions and analysis • substitutions and turnarounds • and more. **Volume 2 includes**: modes and modal frameworks • quartal harmony • extended tertian structures and triadic superimposition • pentatonic applications • coloring "outside" the lines and beyond • and more.
00030458 Volume 1 ....$39.99
00030459 Volume 2 ....$32.99

JAZZOLOGY
THE ENCYCLOPEDIA OF JAZZ THEORY FOR ALL MUSICIANS
by Robert Rawlins and Nor Eddine Bahha
This comprehensive resource covers a variety of jazz topics, for beginners and pros of any instrument. The book serves as an encyclopedia for reference, a thorough methodology for the student, and a workbook for the classroom.
00311167 ....$24.99

MODALOGY
SCALES, MODES & CHORDS: THE PRIMORDIAL BUILDING BLOCKS OF MUSIC
by Jeff Brent with Schell Barkley
Primarily a music theory reference, this book presents a unique perspective on the origins, interlocking aspects, and usage of the most common scales and modes in occidental music. Anyone wishing to seriously explore the realms of scales, modes, and their real-world functions will find the most important issues dealt with in meticulous detail within these pages.
00312274 ....$24.99

THE SOURCE
THE DICTIONARY OF CONTEMPORARY AND TRADITIONAL SCALES
by Steve Barta
This book serves as an informative guide for people who are looking for good, solid information regarding scales, chords, and how they work together. It provides right and left hand fingerings for scales, chords, and complete inversions. Includes over 20 different scales, each written in all 12 keys.
00240885 ....$21.99

Prices, contents & availability subject to change without notice.
0523
068